THE
GHOSTLY TALES
OF
THE
ADIRONDACKS

Published by Arcadia Children's Books
A Division of Arcadia Publishing
Charleston, SC
www.arcadiapublishing.com

Spooky America is a trademark of Arcadia Publishing, Inc.

First published 2022

Manufactured in the United States

ISBN 978-1-4671-9868-4

Library of Congress Control Number: 2022932227

All images courtesy of Shutterstock.com; p. 6 Carol Bell/Shutterstock.com; p. 60 Ritu Manoj Jethani/Shutterstock.com.

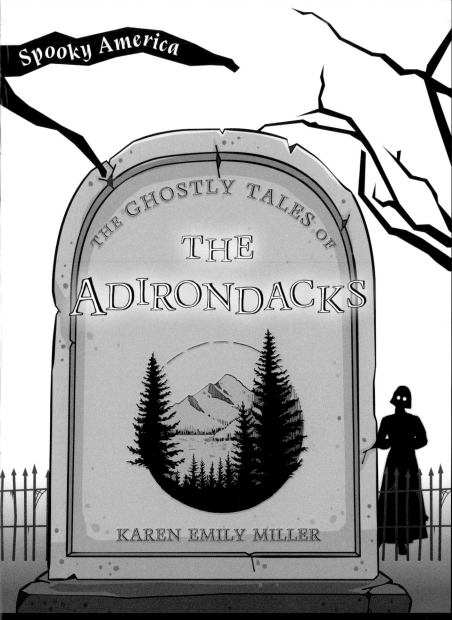

Spooky America

THE GHOSTLY TALES OF

THE ADIRONDACKS

KAREN EMILY MILLER

Adapted from *Haunted Adirondacks* by Dennis Webster

arcadia®
CHILDREN'S BOOKS

VT

MA

CT

Table of Contents & Map Key

Atlantic Ocean

Introduction

Who do you call when you've seen a ghost?

Ghostbusters? No, they were a great team, but unfortunately, not real. The real work of detecting ghosts and supernatural phenomena is done by volunteers called paranormal investigators. They use cutting-edge equipment to detect supernatural activity. Their bag of tricks includes infrared cameras to see in the dark, equipment to measure changes in the

EMF (electromagnetic field), full-spectrum cameras to see sources of light the human eye can't see. They even have equipment that records sounds that the human ear can't hear. With their help, we're going to investigate the ghostly mysteries of the Adirondacks.

People have lived in the Adirondacks since the last Ice Age, which ended about 15,000 BC. Can you imagine how many lives have begun and ended in that time? Happy stories, sad stories, and spooky stories float around the Adirondacks, which covers over five thousand square miles!

Joining a team of paranormal investigators, we'll dig into some of the supernatural mysteries. This time, we won't have rely only on our senses. We'll have equipment the ghostbusters would have loved! Let's go find some ghosts!

Sagamore Resort

The Many Ghosts of the Sagamore Resort

How does it feel to be on a top-ten list? Good. Yes? What if the list is one of haunted hotels? If you're afraid of ghosts, maybe this isn't the place for you. But if you're a ghost hunter, you should visit the Sagamore Resort. Not only is it beautiful, but it has plenty of ghosts to greet you.

There are many reasons for spirits to haunt the Sagamore. The hotel was built on a Native

American burial ground. Battles of the French and Indian War were fought there. There are a lot of restless spirits with nothing to do but haunt you.

The people at the Sagamore aren't shy about their ghosts. When you check in, the receptionist will present you with a list of resident ghosts and even offer you a ghost tour. That's what you signed up for when you decided to visit the Sagamore. You can't wait to begin!

The tour leader, who was raised in a funeral home, is comfortable with ghosts. She says she has seen them many again and again.

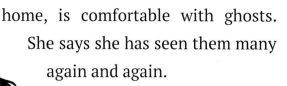

"This way," she says and leads you to an elevator. It's not spooky, like an old-fashioned birdcage elevator. It looks like an ordinary elevator, with buttons on a wall and solid doors. It's the mirrors that make the elevator different from others. Two large identical mirrors face each other. When you look, you see yourself, the mirrored you, yourself, the mirrored self, and on and on to infinity.

That doesn't seem spooky to you, just interesting.

The guide says, "We think this mirrored elevator is the portal the spirits use to go back and forth between their dimension and ours."

You put your finger in the mirror. You look to see if there's a space between your finger and the reflection it makes. If there is one, the mirror might be a portal.

Is there a space, just a tiny one? While you're deciding, your investigatory meters sound off. The first is a "mel meter" that measures temperature and electromagnetism. Temperature measurement is important when you are tracking ghosts. Ghost hunters think a spirit's presence makes the temperature around them drop. That's why, they explain, people get goosebumps. If there's just a small spike in the electromagnetic field and no temperature change, there's probably nothing paranormal.

The "gauss meter" measures the direction and intensity of small magnetic fields. Some say that the conscious minds of humans are made out of an electromagnetic field. They think this field never disintegrates, even when someone dies. The electromagnetic field is what the gauss meter is measuring.

Phew! Something is happening. The gauss meter buzzes, and the EMF reader shows the radiation is fluctuating wildly. All this happening in an elevator!

By the time the elevator door opens, you're wondering if you missed seeing something in the mirrors. Maybe there was a portal there after all.

The tour leader guides you to the hotel kitchen. Everything shines: the stainless steel counters, spoons and ladles hanging from racks. Usually you would see a chef or two preparing meals, chopping and dicing ingredients.

"That's what a chef assistant was doing when one of our ghosts surprised him," says your guide.

"Didn't anyone else see it too?"

"Not at 4:20 in the morning. He was in early, getting ready for breakfast. That's probably why he was blasting rap. He had the place to himself so he wasn't worried about annoying others with loud music."

Chop, chop, chop. He was lost in his rhythm when he heard someone ask, "Whose words are these?"

He looked up. Standing next to him was a woman dressed in a style from the 1930s. Without saying another word, she walked past him and dissolved into a wall. The chef rolled up his knives and walked out of the kitchen and the Sagamore hotel, never to return.

After hearing that story, you're glad there's no music playing.

Next, she takes you to the front desk. You didn't see any ghosts when you checked in, so you don't expect to see any now.

"This isn't the usual time for a haunting," says the guide. "They seem to like the early quiet hours."

She tells you about a hotel manager working the desk in the morning. When the elevator door opened, he was surprised. Who would begin a night out at 1:45 a.m.?

It wasn't an ordinary guest venturing into the lobby. A woman in Victorian dress sashayed past him and through a wall.

A couple dressed in early-1900s party clothes asked two employees if the party in the ballroom was still going on. There was a ballroom but no party. "No, there was no party," the receptionist stammered and watched them walk away. With every step, they faded, until eventually, they disappeared altogether.

There's one ghost that you might not want to meet. It's the spirit of a murdered maid. The maid had been carrying on with a male guest who happened to be married. When the wife found out, she killed the maid by smothering her with a pillow.

Guests often see the spirit of the maid, either in the husband's hotel room itself or just outside of it. Don't attempt a hello, she's too angry to chat.

You decide you'll end your ghost hunt on a happier note.

"Are there any ghosts here that I might like to meet?"

The guide tells you about a boy on the golf course. He had been killed in a car accident in the 1950s.

"Don't' worry about him. I think he likes it here. He must have been naughty in life, for he certainly is in the afterlife."

She said that the boy steals golf balls and then flings them at unsuspecting golfers. It's never a hard-enough throw to hurt anyone. It does startle them, though, and ruins their concentration. She adds, "If you're playing golf and you hear a giggle, duck. He probably just stole a ball and is getting ready to throw it."

So much more to see at the Sagamore. But so little time. It's time to go.

You wonder if you'll spot a Native American ghost walking in the courtyard or bump into one of the children running and skipping down the hallways. You stop outside the spa. A ghost there is said to flush the toilets whenever the water level is low.

A ghost haunter would exhaust himself if he stayed at the Sagamore Resort. However, if he booked a room not shared with a noisy ghost, when he lay his head on the pillow, he'd fall asleep with a smile on his face.

Hauntings at the Brightside Training Center

If someone says the word *brightside*, what do you think of? You might think it's a saying reminding you to face a situation with confidence and hope.

However, if you live by Raquette Lake in the Adirondacks, Brightside calls to mind *haunted*.

Or, if you know local history, you might say, "That's the place where they stored dead people in the hotel basement."

It's actually the third thought that fits the Brightside Learning Center, a hotel on an island on Raquette Lake. The first owner of the hotel served as a coroner for the county. That meant he was in charge of disposing of the dead. Normally, that meant sending bodies to a funeral home for burial or cremation. However, in the 1880s, there were no boats to cross the frozen lake to pick up the dead. Besides, in the winter, the ground in New York State was frozen solid. So, anyone who died on the island, they were buried in the soft dirt in the hotel's cellar. There they stayed until spring.

That's reason enough for the hotel to be haunted. Perhaps, but people say paranormal activity began after a young husband went

missing in a fog. The story says that the husband needed something in town. It was a winter day, so he must have reasoned he could cross the frozen lake safely. Still, his wife worried. She watched him stride into the cold blue haze that covered the lake. She never saw him again. The story continues. The wife was so heartbroken that she died shortly after. In those days, when someone died after losing a loved one, they were said to have died of a broken heart.

That's a good story to tell around a campfire on a summer night. You finish by whispering, "The wife is still there, watching out the window."

Some might laugh. Others nod solemnly. They say they have seen the wife at the window.

Still, you might not be convinced the tale is true.

You're told to talk to one of the construction workers at the hotel. He's been working at Brightside for years. He has a story to tell, too.

One of the repairs he made was in a hotel room just above the kitchen. That was the room where the woman and her husband had stayed.

"I found a lady's coat hanging in the closet. It couldn't have belonged to one of the guests now. It was too old-fashioned. In fact, it looked like a coat someone from the early 1900s might wear."

He goes on to tell you that he didn't give the coat much thought. He says that people often leave things behind. Maybe this coat was forgotten by a guest long ago, and no one bothered to remove it from the closet. So he did. He thought the management might donate it or just throw it away. They said they did, and he didn't give the coat another thought. Then one day, he went back to the room to check on the renovation work. Being a curious fellow, he opened the closet door.

He said he almost dropped his toolbox. In the closet hung two coats. He recognized one

as the old-fashioned lady's coat. The other hung so close to the lady's that it seemed to be embracing it. The coat was one that someone might wear in the early 1900s.

The construction worker was scared. But he also thought it was sweet. It was as if the husband's spirit had returned to keep company with his wife.

Then you have your own ghostly experience. Being a ghost hunter, you ask the owner if you can investigate the hotel. Where do you go first? The basement, of course. That's where all the bodies were buried. You know the bodies were stored there for only a few weeks or months before they were removed. But, you wonder, could there be some ghostly energy left behind?

It's just a minute or two before you feel the supernatural. Your stomach knots. You know you have to leave the cellar or you will be sick.

Once upstairs, you decide to take on a less frightening investigation. There's a small cabin on the grounds of the hotel that is said to be haunted by a woman. People have said they've seen the pale oval of a woman's face at the window.

The tiny house is named the Mother-in-Law's Cabin. It might be called that because it sits away from the main hotel. In the past, elderly parents often went to live with their adult children. If there wasn't a need for the parents to live with the family, a tiny house nearby was a solution to caring for an elderly relative.

That's where you go on that sunny afternoon. The sky is clear, the sun is shining. It's not the time for a haunting.

The cabin is clean if a bit musty, since no one has used it for a long time. The

bed is made with fresh sheets, and the floor has been swept. There are even small jars on the dresser, just as there would be if someone lived there. As you look the cabin over, you decide that it looks as though its occupant just walked out the door . . . a hundred years ago.

It's such a pleasant room that you lay down on the bed. Maybe a nap will take away your stomach ache. Minutes pass. Your stomach feels better. You relax. Why not try to communicate with the spirit that is supposed to live here?

You have almost drifted off to sleep when the mood in the cabin changes. The stuffy atmosphere is replaced by something heavy, expectant. It's almost as if someone there wants to reach out and touch you. Suddenly, a jar on the dresser scoots across the top. It stops just before it clatters to the floor.

You've had an exhausting experience in the hotel cellar. You don't want to see who or what is with you. Keeping your eyes shut, you say, "Give me a name."

You don't want to be impolite, for you have heard that spirits don't like to tell their given name.

You add the word "please." You repeat your request.

When you hear a soft whisper, "Emily," right next to you, you let out a whoosh of breath. You hadn't realized you had been holding it.

"Thank you," you manage to whisper. You are alone in the cabin. You have no paranormal equipment, no teammates.

After a time, the heavy air dissolves. You sense the spirit has left. So, you decide, you will, too.

When you report to the owner what has happened, he smiles.

"Emily," he says, "is a woman who was a regular guest at our hotel. Everyone enjoyed her company. I suppose the spirit in the cabin must have liked her, too."

That's when you tell the owner, "Thank you," and board a boat to the mainland. You've experienced enough of this day to call the investigation to an end, at least for now.

Brightside, a beautiful hotel and gathering place, has taught you a lesson.

Even ghosts can have favorites, just like the living.

The Stagecoach
Inn, Lake Placid

You should have known. The paranormal team told you the inn is a hub of paranormal activity. It doesn't surprise you. The inn had been a meeting place for town residents and visitors for over 150 years. Not only is it a place to sleep, but you can get mail and provisions here, too. It was even a stagecoach stop before the trains started arriving in the area in 1893. With all those souls passing through, it's no wonder there are a few who stayed behind.

You've been given a room that is supposed to be quiet, peaceful. It's snowing outside. Since the inn is closed that weekend, you're alone in the inn except for the innkeeper, who has a room on the other side of the building.

Alone in a haunted inn in the middle of winter? Why not? You're a ghost hunter!

You open your closet. There's a sturdy hanger with a lantern tied to it. Sliding it aside, you hang your coat and put down your travel bag.

You take a few minutes to write in your journal. You're eager to write down your thoughts and settle in.

Suddenly, a "thump" comes from the closet. When you open it, you see the hanger and lantern upright on the floor. It's not broken or even cracked. Maybe it's a spirit telling you not to move his stuff.

When the innkeeper comes to take you on a tour, wearing rosary beads on your neck. Catholics uses rosary beads to mark their prayers, but for some ghost hunters, they are used as a kind of protection against evil spirits or vampires.

When you tell the innkeeper about the jumping lantern, she laughs. "That's what happens in a spooky inn." She tells you about the most recent paranormal activity.

A rattling door awakened guests on the second floor. After the doorknob started turning, they leapt out of bed and flung open the door. Nothing was there but an empty hallway.

The housekeeper and owner agree, the

ghosts like watching television. One afternoon while the housekeeper vacuumed, she was startled by the blare of the TV. It was even louder than her vacuum! She turned it off. The ghosts were more persistent the next time they tried to watch. The inn's owner had a showdown with them. She'd click it off, only to hear it click on moments later.

Finally, she said, "Please don't do this to me." She said she was okay with ghosts being in the inn. However, she didn't want to see any of them. This time when she turned it off, it stayed off.

"Let me tell you about the pink roses," the innkeeper says as she shows you to her

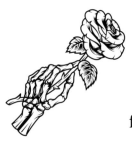

quarters. She tells you that she loves fresh flowers and had bought pink roses to sit on top of her dresser. Their fragrance filled the room, and their petals shone with color. She wanted to remember this gorgeous bouquet, so she took several pictures of it. Later, when she looked at the photos, she saw a surprise appearance. In one of them, the ghostly image of a lady leaned over the roses, appearing to enjoy their sweet scent. In the fashion of the past, she wore a hat on her head.

The rest of your ghost-hunting team arrives. It doesn't take long for them to have the same experiences you already had. One member feels odd, out of sorts, when he inspects the Day Room. You tell him that you also felt strange there. When another teammate checks your closet, he feels cold chills run up and down the back of his neck. A third member confesses to you that the night before, she had dreamed about you in the inn. An entity, an orb or mist, she doesn't say which, circled above you as you slept.

Excited, you oversee the paranormal equipment being set up. This place is full of ghosts! Your investigation starts in the room that gave you shivers. You volunteer to lie down on the bed. "All the better to breathe, relax, and get ready for the spirits," you say.

A few moments after you lie down, a heavy weight settles on your chest.

"Shush, don't move. It's only a child," says one of your team.

You wait patiently. The weight isn't too bad, and you hope the rest of them can record the haunting. After a few minutes, the weight lifts. The child is gone, you're told.

When the child goes, she leaves someone behind. There's an entity, a presence, lurking behind the camera. When we leave the room, it seems to follow us.

One of our group gets poked in the back, and another smells a burning cigar.

The mel meter sounds off as soon as you step onto the threshold of the second floor. Since it measures both temperature and electromagnetic changes, it's helpful for detecting ghosts.

Our next tool, the dowsing rods, show a supernatural presence. You're glad someone thought to bring their rods. Although old-fashioned, your team has found them helpful in contacting ghosts.

People think of digging wells when you mention "dowsing rods. " The L-shaped rods have been used since ancient times to find sources of energy. Dowsers have used them find both water and minerals. Ghost hunters use them to find the electromagnetic energy ghosts give off.

You finish off your first night of investigation by going into the basement. Like most basements, you discover spirits. The Stagecoach Inn has an entity who skitters away every time on of your team approaches.

The next night has some surprises, and they aren't all good. Your first experience is pleasant. A little girl ghost peeks at you from around the corner at the top of the stairs. You try to guess her name. After a few mistakes, you decide her name is Mary. Later, you discover that in the mid- 1800s, a girl aged six had died near the Stagecoach Inn. Her name was Mary Osgood.

As you retrace your steps to the second floor, a male spirit seems to follow. He doesn't interfere, so you are content to let him trail behind. When you go into the innkeeper's quarters, the entity changes. The team had placed a fresh bouquet on the dresser to draw out the lady ghost who had admired them before. Two of our team sits down on the innkeeper's bed to wait for something to happen. It does.

The blanket on the bed begins to ripple. Starting at the foot of the bed, it slowly makes its way up to where your friends sit. They shriek. You act. These are your co-workers, and you're going to help them. Suddenly, you feel the rosary being ripped from your neck. At the same time, one of your friends opens her eyes. Inches away from her face is a male ghost.

You make your way to another guest room. It's time for a break. You all need one. Once there, you repair your rosary and string it around your neck. The handheld detector springs to life, buzzing and showing surges in electromagnetic activity. Could the energy be coming from Mary? The presence does not seem to be angry.

"There's a painting of a dog downstairs," you say. "It's a brown puppy with a white blaze on his chest. Do you remember the puppy's name, Mary?"

As before, we have a hard time understanding her. We try the names "Marty" and "Molly" with no success. Somehow we guess the name "Magnolia." That's it.

The night's work is finished. When you climb back into your bed, you turn on ghost-detecting equipment. You'd like to be alerted if any of the spirits try to visit you. Even though the door is shut and locked, you know a wooden barrier is no trouble for a cross to pass through.

Sometime during the night, your detectors buzz and glow the red, yellow, and green to tell you a spirit is near. You, however, are so tired, you turn them off. You snuggle back under the covers. The next morning, you're rested and pleased with how the investigation has gone. You're feeling fine.

The same can't be said for your rosary. It lies on the floor. It has been ripped apart. You're not frightened, though. Next time you enter a haunted house, you'll ask permission to bring along your rosary. Just like people, spirits have opinions and will express them if there is something they don't like, and you've got to respect that.

CHAPTER 4

Séance at the Woodgate Free Library

Sometimes ghost hunters don't use equipment. Who needs a special camera when you can see and hear books flying off the shelf? That's what happened when you visit the tiny free library in Woodgate, New York. You've come for an old-fashioned ghost raising, and you get it!

There have been many paranormal investigations in the library over the years.

Ghost hunters have uncovered evidence of the supernatural. This time, a séance is going to be the way to discover spirits.

You've come to see Clara Hubert, a girl who was in the building when it was a school. You know you'll be able to identify her, for she's one of the students in the 1915 school photo.

However, you're going to keep your eyes and ears open, as it is said that Clara's not the only spirit roaming the two-room building.

Before you can start the séance, the library's director warns you not to sit close to the library bookshelves. Big, heavy books have flown off the shelves. Something has been tossing them, but no one knows who or why.

Perhaps because she wants to test your psychic ability, she asks if anyone in your group knows the name of the third book that's usually tossed. The first two are weighty cookbooks.

The third book. *Hmm*. You wonder to yourself. Then a name pops into your head ... a book about Harry Truman, who was president of the United States from 1945–1953.

"That's it," says the director.

Maybe that's the sign the director was waiting for: an assurance one of our group is spiritually able to participate in the séance.

Shortly after, you're herded to a round table. You're told to sit down and interlock your hands with the people sitting beside you.

"Don't let go of your neighbor's hand," you are warned. "It's the collective energy of the group that calls forth the spirits."

A Saint David's candle is lit and placed in the middle of the table. It's a candle often used in séances. Some people call it the corpse candle. It is supposed to help draw in the ghosts.

The rest of the room is dark. You can't even see shadows! Ever since the nineteenth century, when séances began, no bright lights have been permitted. It's only after the spirit had made a visit that stronger light is allowed.

"Spirits don't like light," you're told.

A bowl of unlit sage is placed nearby. If the spirits are threatening, the séance leader can drive them away by burning sage. It's a practice used to combat ghosts since ancient times.

You look around the table. The surrounding dark seems to drape over all of you. The only evidence that you are in the twenty-first century is the ghost hunting equipment: a tripod, a digital recorder, and a few handheld devices to record sounds.

You chant, in unison, a prayer to invite the spirits. You begin to sweat. Is it because it's a hot, humid night in August? Or are you afraid you might be hit by a book?

Everyone around the table is staring into the dark corners of the room. Each one seems to be in his own world. You tighten your grip on you partners' hands and wait.

But not for long. You feel a cold breath against the back of your neck. There are muffled voices, just low enough so you can't understand what's being said. Footsteps sound, but you see nothing in the shadows.

Is that a giggle you hear? A whisper? Next, you hear the sound of pages turning, as if someone is riffling through a big book.

You tense, ready yourself to break the circle if a book falls off the shelf. The rustling and whispering lasts for almost forty-five minutes. Then as abruptly as it began, it ends.

You all chant the prayer again, this time asking the spirits to leave. A shroud of sadness settles. One by one, your group files out of the room.

Later, you gather together to try to make sense of what happened.

"Look at this," someone says, pointing to a sticker affixed to one of the bookcases. "It says, 'Property of Utica State Hospital.'"

You find a few more. Many of the bookshelves were donated by the hospital, called "Old Main" by the locals. Old Main was the ending place for unfortunates judged insane or dangerous.

You remember something you learned on an earlier ghost hunt. Objects can have ghosts attached to them, much like shadows seem stuck to your body. What if you were one of  the inmates, sentenced to spend the rest of your life in an insane asylum? Could your sadness and desperation seep into the wood of the bookshelves?

As you leave the library, you're relieved you didn't see little Clara. She might have stayed behind to relive the happiness of her school days. Maybe, you hope, the giggles belonged to her. As for the rest, you are relieved you left them behind.

Van Auken's Inne

If you want to meet the friendliest of spirits, hop off the Adirondack Scenic Train at the town of Thendara. Its hotel, the Van Auken's Inne, has been operating since 1894, when lumber was king in the United States. The rich forests nearby provided plenty of timber for our growing country. The town boasted a sawmill and a way to ship it all over the country. What could be easier for the lumber companies to send the timber on its way? You can't do better than having the railroad run through the middle of town.

Thendara, then called Fulton Chain, had a hotel just for them. The hotel was built in 1891, just in time for the flood of lumberjacks who came to town. That's where visitors and workers went to get supplies and catch up on local gossip. It must have been a friendly place, as some of the guests and hotel workers never left.

The inn itself has had several owners. First called Mack's Hotel, then Wakely's, the hotel got its final name of Van Auken's Inne in 1904. That was when the Van Auken family bought the hotel and moved it away from

the railroad tracks. Sparks from the train engines were too big a fire hazard to the wooden Victorian.

Don't worry that ghosts were left behind when the inn moved. What was 75 feet to a spirit dedicated to stay at the hotel?

When you go to the inn, you'll be guaranteed delicious food, a fine bed, and a good time, if you remember not to disturb the spirits. The ghosts like things to stay the same. They will let you know if you upset their routine.

What brings you and fellow paranormal investigators to the inn? You've received a request from the owners. They want you to determine if the inn is haunted or just an old building that squeaks and groans with age.

The first thing you notice as you pull up to the inn is the scent of pine trees. The smell, tangy and sharp, greets you as you climb the steps to the hotel. Stately pillars line its wide porch that seems made for rocking chairs. Nearby, the whistle of the Adirondack Scenic Train whistles. The Van Auken Inne is a regular stop for tourists. Why not? It's so warm and welcoming . . . at first.

It doesn't take long to hear disturbing stories from the inn's workers. One woman said a spirit sidled up to her and whispered, "Hello," into her ear. A bartender left, never to return, after someone or something, invisible to the eye, rearranged things. The spirit moved glasses, cups, anything small and light, as he watched. Was it a poltergeist who turned radios on and off? If they were equipped with motion detectors, they'd flicker on, even though no one was standing nearby. Even Christmas decorations misbehaved.

There's a lot to see here. The owners say there's paranormal activity all over the hotel, upstairs and downstairs. Your team splits up. Some of you go to the basement, where the owners recreated a speakeasy. Speakeasys were popular during the 1930s when people were banned from buying and selling liquor. The law didn't stop those who wanted to drink liquor, and the speakeasy was born. It's called "speakeasy" because customers were told to speak softly there. No one wanted the police to find them.

Is the speakeasy a reason for ghosts to complain? No one knows for sure. Ghost hunters say that paranormal activity increases when a repair is done in old places. They think that the ghosts don't like change—any change at all.

Maybe there are spirits at the speakeasy because they enjoy having a drink? You decide.

You're in the group who investigates the basement. You feel a cold chill as soon as you descend the stairs. A woman, an experienced investigator and sensitive to the paranormal, is struck with a terrible headache and has to leave.

You don't have to wait long to sense something strange. As you search the basement, a shadowy figure follows you, darting out of sight as soon as you get close.

"This is full of spirits," you say, after another on your team feels the presence of a nun. A nun in a speakeasy? Maybe she arrived at the inn before the bar was built. Your fellow ghost seeker says the nun, named Sarah, is lonely. No wonder spirits make themselves known, you think. They must want company!

Everyone hears voices in the shadows. Did the voices tell you to go to the root cellar? You aren't sure. However, your team agrees to investigate it.

You aren't disappointed when you get there. Waiting for

you is a little boy ghost, half hidden in a corner. Your paranormal equipment picks up his name. He tells you that his name is Matthew, but doesn't say how he died or why he has chosen to stay. Matthew makes the meters and flashlights turn on and off. You guess he must be bored and wants you to play with him. Not too frightening, you think to yourself. Still, when he brushes up next to you, chills run up and down your back. For a moment, you wish he'd chose someone else to visit.

The rest of your team tackles Rooms 8, 9, and 12 because they are said to haunted.

"Room 8 terrified me as soon as I walked in," said a team member. Everyone agrees, saying they felt chilled as soon as they set foot in the room. After the initial shock of the cold, a blanket of misery covered them.

What could have happened here?" They asked each other. Later, they found there was a reason for sadness to fill the room. A man had died in the bathroom.

What about those who attached themselves to the inn because they were happy there?

Matthew, the curious little spirit, might have been one. But there's no doubt the ghost Charlie loved his time there. Both of your

teams run into Charlie again and again as you walk the halls. His spirit is bright and lively. Instead of giving you goosebumps, he makes you chuckle.

If you want to see Charlie, too, ask to see a photo taken in the early 1900s. The staff and the guests line the porch, smiling, happy to be there. There's one figure that stands out from the rest of the crowd. He's the only one dressed all in white. That's Charlie, making his presence known.

According to reports, he's still doing that. He's a friendly fellow, so when you bump into him, don't run away. Just say "Hello, good to see you. I like it here, too!"

Fort William Henry

Flowers for the Dead at Fort William Henry

It's not surprising that a place of battle holds shadows of fear, anger, and desperation. Fort William Henry was built as staging place from which to attack the French, who battled with the British for dominance of the new frontier. On August 7, 1757, an army of over six thousand French and their Native American allies attacked the two thousand three hundred soldiers and families who sheltered there.

Although the French had promised a peaceful surrender, their allies had not. They didn't acknowledge the European rules of war. Those who didn't die in the battle died when the enemy set fire to the fort. A few, unlucky or lucky ones, you wonder, were taken captive. No wonder the fort held terrible memories. The present fort was built upon the ashes of the old one, and some say that it holds the residue of the tragedy.

Picture yourself as a soldier, defending Fort William Henry at Lake George in New York in 1757. How would you feel moments before an enemy fired upon you? Some of the musket balls might bury themselves in the wooden wall  that separates you from the attackers. Some might pierce the bodies of your fellow soldiers. You lift your musket, peer through a hole in the fort, aim, and fire. The force of the musket's explosion of ammunition knocks you back a foot or two. You hope your shot hits its mark, but can't see clearly. All you can see is a mob of the white uniforms of the French and the faces of the Abenaki and Caughnawaga warriors.

Now, imagine yourself as a tourist, over 250 years later, stopping by the fort for an afternoon of fun. Fort William Henry has many volunteers reenacting the life and death of the fort. You brush by red-coated soldiers and women and children dressed in the homespun dress of the time. Far off, you see the actors who play the French and the Native American allies gather together for a pretend attack.

The re-enactors have experiences to share with you. "I often smell baking bread," says one. "Which is impossible since there are no working ovens. Others have smelled tobacco, even perfume when no one is about."

Another says, "I've seen men in red coats playing cards. When I look again, they're gone."

Still another reports, "One night when I slept over in the bunk room, I heard voices and footsteps. I thought I was the only one there, so I jumped out of bed. I wanted to see whoever it was who was playing a trick on me. When I opened the door, no one was there. No person could have gotten away so quickly."

"If you want to feel a ghost, go to one of the

fortified rooms below ground. People have seen a little girl by the benches. We leave flowers for her. We think she likes them because when they are there, she often visits."

That's what you have come to see—ghosts. You wonder why a child's spirit would haunt a place where soldiers fired their muskets and rifles. Perhaps the child had belonged to one of the families who sheltered there.

You make you way to one of the casement rooms. These rooms ringed the fort. They had tiny peepholes for inserting your musket so

you could fire in relative safety. You were safe unless the musket balls pierced the wall or the cannon balls exploded through.

You see a vase of flowers on one of the benches and sit there. After a moment, you feel a cold, clammy cloud settle on your right side. You were told that you'd feel her presence on whatever side she chose to sit.

"Are you the little girl? Can you tell me your name?"

Out of the cold fog comes a voice, light and high.

"Abigail."

You sit silently, not wanting to disturb her. After a time, the clamminess is gone, and so, you think, is Abigail.

If you want to visit Fort William Henry and meet Abigail, be sure to take some flowers with you.

CHAPTER 7

The Toboggan Inn

Who'd guess that sprucing up a hotel would shake loose ghosts? Does tearing down and breaking through walls free the spirits? Are they so happy at having a chance to roam that they behave badly? Is that why they throw plates, push chairs, and even scold people and tell them to hush?

That seems to be the case at the Toboggan Inn in Eagle Bay.

In the past, the building was an office for the railroad, a restaurant with apartments above, and a cafe. The original building was constructed in the early 1900s and needed repairs. As soon as the first wall was torn down, the ghosts burst out of the hiding places. There was so much paranormal activity that the owners kept a logbook. There they recorded ghostly footsteps, chatter in empty rooms and unearthly whispers.

Everyone hoped that when the renovations were completed, the activity would stop. The ghosts, though, kept misbehaving.

That's why you're at the Toboggan Inn tonight. The owners want to make sure that the ghostly activity won't hurt anyone.

You're setting up your tripod for a camera when a clatter of silverware startles you. Next, a dinner plate whizzes by your head. You're so surprised, you almost knock over a cup of dimes that sits on the counter.

"Don't worry about the cup," says the owner. "That's where we keep the dimes we find in the inn. They pop up everywhere. We don't know where they come from or who put them down."

You finish setting up the paranormal equipment and report to Ghost Central. That's any place away from the investigation where you keep track of the team's work. Their cameras and meters feed information to the monitors that you have set in front of you.

It doesn't take long for the ghosts appear. In the basement, one researcher makes contact with a little boy named Samuel or Simon. She's not sure which. The child tells them that his favorite game is "Simon Says."

"He seems happy we're here," your teammate says. "He's patted me several times."

That information tells you that Simon, or Samuel, probably isn't the ghost who throws dishes or scolds people.

The team in the dining room don't find the angry ghost either. The ghost there stroked their hair and patted, ever so lightly, their necks.

So, who is the troublemaker? You think you have the answer when you survey the second floor. There, the spirit is not in a good mood. The members feel a sense of anger and irritation. When Simon/Samuel stays behind as they climb the stairs to the second floor, you wonder if the grumpy ghost frightens him.

There is another spirit who is cranky. In the bar, a lady's voice scolds, "Stay quiet!" Visitors

to the inn remember times they have heard a woman say, "Shush!" Stunned into silence, they turn to look at the prickly lady. No one is there.

After you pack up the equipment, you wonder if you and your team have aggravated the ghosts. Door open and shut, a toy piano plunks out a tune, and ectoplasm appear on the security cameras.

"The Toboggan Inn is haunted," you say. However, no one from the team has been

injured. The owner's son said he was scratched, but that's the worst of it People have been lectured to, yes. Had dishes thrown at them? Yes. But no one is badly hurt. You wonder if the ghosts don't want to hurt anyone. They might just want to aggravate! You decide you'll return, for the food is good. And you might find dimes to add to your collection of paranormal souvenirs.

Rhinelander Estate in Speculator, Lake Pleasant

Beautiful wife. Beautiful ghosts. That's the beginning and almost the end of this sad story near the village of Speculator in the town of Lake Pleasant, New York.

Mr. Rhinelander seemed to have everything. He was one of the founders of the town and owned three hundred acres of forest on Elm

Lake. He built a mansion on the hillside for his wife, Mary. Nothing was left out. There was a barn, a stable, and servants' quarters. He wanted it to be so beautiful that Mary would never want to leave. Actually, that was the problem. He didn't want Mary to leave because he was jealous of everyone else. He didn't even like people looking at her. People say that is why they left New York City. Mary had friends and family there, and he didn't want to share her with anyone.

But Mary was miserable. The mansion on Elm Lake was isolated. Mary was alone except for Phillip and the servants. It was dangerous to become her friend. A washerwoman's body was found floating along the shoreline. A peddler, people said, was murdered by Phillip. Some said he threw the poor man's body down a well on the estate.

Not only was Mary far from everyone she loved, she was forbidden to make friends in town. Whenever she ventured into town,

Phillip had to be at her side. He didn't want anyone to look at her, only himself.

Mary tried to keep in touch with her friends and family with letters. But when she gave them to her husband, he destroyed them.

That's the story people tell about Rhinelander Estate. Mary died three years after moving to the mansion. Rumors flew. Some thought Phillip had poisoned her. No one knows.

Phillip built a stone vault on the mansion grounds and placed Mary there.

After Mary was gone, Phillip eventually tired of the mansion. He left his estate and the town five years later. The house stood empty and abandoned. Caretakers came to watch over the land and the house. That is when the hauntings began or, at least, when they were reported.

Mary's spirit appeared to the caretakers many times. It was clear that the Rhinelanders had not left the mansion after all.

Sometimes Mary would visit the caretakers if they slept in her old room. One caretaker was roused from sleep by a woman's sobbing. She opened her eyes and saw Mary sitting in a chair close to the bed. When she opened her eyes, she saw the spirit of Mary, crying, tears running down her cheeks.

Another caretaker caught a glimpse of Mary sitting idly, stroking her hair. The children of the caretakers said they saw floating candles. Perhaps it was the spirit of the washerwoman, still collecting clothes to wash. Or maybe it was Mary herself.

Phillip, even in afterlife, wouldn't leave Mary. Heavy boots, like the ones a man would wear stomping about outside, were often heard going up and down stairs.

Finally, the mansion was abandoned. Not even caretakers walked the halls. Mary stayed, that's what curious visitors said. They claimed they saw her looking out a bedroom window. Others didn't have the experience of seeing Mary. They did hear the wails of a child from deep inside the house.

The hauntings have never ended, even after the mansion burned down to the ground. People were curious. They came to see the ruins, curious about the story of the imprisoned wife. Those who came camped within the foundations of the house heard footsteps and saw strange orbs floating in the woods nearby. Everyone who stayed overnight remarked on the sadness that overtook them during their stay.

The prospect of haunted ruins is what draws you to the Rhinelander Estate. You plan only to make a short trip, so you pack only two paranormal devices. You take you a handheld ghost meter and a digital recorder.

As it happens, you didn't need either one to convince you of a paranormal visit. You experience it.

It's a hot July afternoon, so you are surprised that the temperature drops as soon as you step on estate grounds. "Why not ask a question now?," you murmur. "There is something going on here."

You ask, "Is Mary there?"

Soon you realize that someone, or something, *is* there with you. The wind stops blowing. The birds still. The squirrels stop their skittering on the forest floor. You close your eyes, trying to make sense of what is happening.

That's when you hear it: a woman's whisper from about twenty feet away. When the words stop, you whip around to see who was speaking to you. There's no one.

You wonder if you can contact Phillip. Again, you ask aloud your question. "Did you love Mary?" Uh-oh. A wave of sorrow sweeps over you. Wrong question, you decide, at least for Phillip. Still, you press on. "I heard Mary was beautiful." Another mistake, this time a big one. Your heart races, and your right eye itches and stings. A new emotion, despair, hits you hard. You decide to lie down and rest. You need to regroup and get yourself back together.

You hear footsteps. They are not the stomping of boots, but the light footfalls of a child or woman. You don't want to scare the spirit away. The steps stop about a foot away, so you keep your eyes shut, even though you would like to look. If you did, would you see Mary's ghost?

Somehow you sense that it would be the wrong thing to do. Perhaps Phillip, even as a ghost, didn't want anyone looking at his wife. You don't want to endanger her spirit.

Something ridiculous happens. A loud, obnoxious pig grunt blasts the air on your left side. There's another one, this time closer. Your handheld ghost meter sounds. You have to open your eyes. What is happening?

When you look, you see nothing but the house foundation and surrounding forest. It must be a residual haunting, you decide. Of course, there had been livestock on the estate.

First, there had been a barn, Also, a place as isolated as the Rhinelander Estate probably kept animals for food. Why go into the town to a butcher if you could keep your meat close by?

So, you reason, the pig grunts were ghostly memories from the past. Just like Mary, imprisoned on the estate, never to leave.

Your mood lifts the moment you step over the property line. As you walk away, you wish Mary were with you, leaving the sadness and

despair behind. Let Phillip roam there alone. He deserves the emptiness. Mary does not.

So, Mary's story hasn't ended. Perhaps someday her spirit can leave the estate once and for all. You hope so.

Spirits of the
Hotel Saranac

Ghost hunting in the Adirondacks takes you
many places—a decayed factory, an Army fort,
and even a two-room library. They are all home
to spirits. So when you arrive at Hotel Saranac
for an investigation, you smile. Hotel Saranac
is a one-of-a-kind hotel. Its second-floor
lobby is modeled after a Venetian palace. It's
famous for its luxury. It boasted one hundred
baths at a time when hotel guests usually

shared one bathroom with everyone else on the floor. It was the first fireproof hotel in the area because it's built of steel, concrete, and brick. Most buildings constructed during the same time were wood and would often burn down. This hotel is also famous for something that doesn't cost money. Hotel Saranac is a six-story assortment of ghosts. Take your pick from spirits in the basement, grand lobby, and the hotel rooms.

You and your paranormal team are arriving in the midst of a renovation. You've learned that ghosts stir when walls come down. But why is the hotel so haunted? One thought is that it is because it's built upon the ashes of a local high school. Ghost hunters think that spirits are drawn to places of great emotion. The fiery destruction of a school would certainly be a catastrophe. Another thought is that ghosts who came to the hotel while living found the Saranac so pleasing, they chose to stay on forever.

What's different about the ghosts at Saranac? First of all, there's a ghost cat. An elderly resident went to sleep one night, folded her hands neatly over the covers, and never woke up. That wouldn't be a tragic way to die, you think. Ask the cat who was sleeping with her mistress. Perhaps he was traumatized when his owner didn't wake up.

No one knows what happened to the cat after the owner died. Everyone knows, though, what happened to the cat in the afterlife. He took up residence in his old room. Guests who stay in the room hear unearthly yowls. A cat's claws make scratches on walls even though no one has seen a cat anywhere near the room. Even stranger are the impressions of a cat left on the neatly made hotel bed.

Another spirit that sets the Saranac apart is the man wearing a top hat. He's dressed in tuxedo and tails. People say the ghost is the spirit of the man who worked at the high school in the early 1900s. The man was said to love his job, so maybe he just decided to stay forever in the place the school used to be! Since the hotel is built partially on the foundation of the burnt-down school, he'd have access to the hotel. Reports say the man was fun-loving and rarely missed a party. Hotel Sarnac has endless parties for him. He can dance away into eternity.

You don't know what to expect on the night of your investigation. Maybe you'll bump into ghostly partygoers. Or you might meet smartly dressed guests from New York City, fated to extend their hotel stay to forever.

You won't have expected a ghost bully, a shy shadow, or a muscle-man spirit. That's what you get, though.

One of your team is pinned to a wall, unable to move even a finger. Another is trailed by a shadow who hides behind a pillar by the kitchen door. Finally, a heavy-weight tripod and video camera are knocked to the floor. That might seem to be an impossible feat. It wouldn't be difficult for a person. However, paranormal researchers say that moving even a glass or plate requires a great deal of spirit energy. Pushing over a tripod and camera would require a super ghost.

The second investigation doesn't disappoint. The ghost cat reappears, a spirit moves the top hat that's stored in the basement, and an investigator discovers what happens if a ghost doesn't like you.

One of the team found he couldn't catch his breath. Seeing him struggle to breathe, the others asked if one of the ghosts was causing the trouble. The spirit answered yes, it was he. No one knows why, but the spirit said he didn't like the team member.

How did they know this? They used a pendulum, a tool often used in ghost hunting. It's a simple technique. First, you ask a spirit to show a "yes." Once the pendulum consistently swings in a repeated pattern, you learn what a "yes" looks like. You then figure out what a "no" when you see a different pattern. That's what the member did and was told the ghost wanted him gone. He might not have needed to ask, though. The spirit knocked a temperature gauge out of his hand. That was all the convincing he needed. He ran out of the room.

CHAPTER
10

Bigfoot, Ohio, New York

Many places say they are the home of Bigfoot. In fact, every state in America claim he roams in their backcountry. Some people say he's a gentle beast. Others think he's a dangerous predator. The Adirondacks Bigfoot is said to be a cranky one.

Stories of this giant hairy humanoid have been told for generations. The Native American first settlers of this area include tales of Bigfoot in their first stories.

In the early 1600s, the French explorer Samuel de Champlain explored the region, looking for rich land to claim for France. He made friends with the Huron people, and they shared their history and folktales with him. They told him of a hairy giant called the Gougou. They warned de Champlain to stay away from the beast. If anyone got too close, the Gougou would hiss and throw rocks.

How could a ten-foot-tall beast hide in New York State? The Adirondacks make it easy. Adirondack Park has a dense forest that spans

millions of acres. Its population is clustered around the big cities. That leaves plenty of room for Bigfoot.

Let's imagine you've come to Ohio, New York, to help a friend. You're not looking for spirits this time. Your friend says something is in the woods near his home.

"My entire crop of blueberries is gone," he says. "I've seen something big moving in the woods."

Both of you agree it must be a black bear. They love blueberries! When you catch scent of something nauseating, you are certain. It's a combination of vomit, poop, and sweat. That's the signature scent of a black bear.

You make a foolproof plan to discover the thief.

"We'll fill a five-gallon pail with raw meat," you say. "No black bear could refuse that treat."

"I have a trail camera that's infrared," says your friend.

You nod. It's a good idea. An infrared camera detects and measures the infrared energy of every object, including bears. The camera converts the infrared data into electronic images. You'll be able to see the bear as it feeds.

After you secure the camera on a sturdy tripod and aim it towards the pail, you leave. Nothing will happen during the day. Bears hunt at sunrise and dusk.

"We'll wait for a few days, give the bear plenty of time to find his treat," you say.

It takes patience to wait, but it's worth it. When you return to the bucket, you find a surprise. The pail stands upright. That doesn't make sense. A bear would knock over the pail to get to the meat.

"Something's not right," you say. "Let's see what the camera shows."

The picture is blurry and smudged. What you see is no bear nor human. It was a Bigfoot who enjoyed your bucket of meat.

There's no mistaking the image. Hairy, big and standing upright—it's a Sasquatch, Gougou, Bigfoot. You can choose any of its names to call it. The humanoid shape is big, bigger than most people. It stands in front of a tree with a knot in its trunk. You measure the distance between the ground and the tree knot. It's eight feet.

Could there be any more Bigfoots close by? As a matter of fact, the town of Whitehall, also in New York State, has reported so many sightings that they celebrate the beast. Every fall, the town holds a festival with speakers, music, tasty treats, and a Bigfoot-calling contest.

No one is sure what a Sasquatch sounds like. Some say it's a howl long and drawn out. Others say it's like a short scream. Still others say it's a low-pitched grunt.

People have fun trying to mimic Bigfoot. How exciting it would be to call one to your side, they think. You decide, though, seeing one by infrared is as close as you want to get. You'd much rather face a grumpy ghost than a shy Bigfoot. Ghosts might leave a scratch or two, but an eight-foot-tall Sasquatch? You'd rather not find out.

Conclusion

You've had quite a journey. Judgmental ghosts, jealous ghosts, sad ghosts—you've experienced them all. You've even crossed over into area that few ghost hunters ever venture into—the dimension of paranormal beasts. The Adirondacks are known for its landscape of 2000 lakes, millions of acres of forests, hotels of luxury and charm. Now you know there is much more than the travel books will tell you. So, next time someone tells you they are traveling to the Adirondacks, tell them about the adventures they won't find on a woodland trail or canoe ride. Who would want to miss out on a ghost adventure?

Karen Emily Miller has been writing about strange creatures since she was six, so writing about the paranormal is a perfect fit. She just moved to Iowa City and is excited to meet those ghosts.

Check out some of the other Spooky America titles available now!

Spooky America was adapted from the creeptastic Haunted America series for adults. Haunted America explores historical haunts in cities and regions across America. Each book chronicles both the widely known and less-familiar history behind local ghosts and other unexplained mysteries. Here's more from *Haunted Adirondacks* author Dennis Webster: